Contents

BAKER'S ONE BOWL
Million Dollar Fudge

Prep: 25 min. | Total: 25 min. | Makes: 60 servings, 1 piece each.

What you need

½ cup butter or margarine

4½ cups sugar

1 can (12 oz.) evaporated milk

3 pkg. (12 oz. each) **BAKER'S** Semi-Sweet Chocolate Chunks

1 jar (7 oz.) **JET-PUFFED** Marshmallow Creme

3 cups **PLANTERS** Chopped Pecans

1 tsp. salt

1 tsp. vanilla

Make It

BRING butter, sugar and milk to full rolling boil in large saucepan on medium heat, stirring constantly. Boil an additional 5 min., stirring constantly.

REMOVE from heat. Gradually add chocolate chunks, stirring until chocolate is completely melted after each addition. Add remaining ingredients; mix well.

POUR into 15×10×1-inch pan sprayed with cooking spray. Cool completely.

To make Rocky Road Fudge, prepare as directed, stirring 2 cups JET-PUFFED Miniature Marshmallows into the hot fudge mixture before pouring into pan.

Vanilla Snowflake Cake

Prep: 45 min. | Total: 2 hr 15 min. (incl. cooling) | Makes: 16 servings.

What you need

- 1 pkg. (2-layer size) yellow cake mix
- 2 pkg. (3.4 oz. each) **JELL-O** Vanilla Flavor Instant Pudding, divided
- 6 oz. **BAKER'S** White Chocolate
- ¼ cup powdered sugar
- 1 cup cold milk
- 1 tub (8 oz.) **COOL WHIP** Whipped Topping, thawed
- ¼ cup raspberry jam, warmed, strained

Make It

HEAT oven to 350°F.

PREPARE cake batter and bake as directed on package for 2 (9-inch) round layers, blending 1 pkg. dry pudding mix into batter before pouring into prepared pans. Cool cakes in pans 10 min.; invert onto wire racks. Gently remove pans; cool cakes completely.

MEANWHILE, draw 3 or 4 snowflake shapes on paper, ranging in size from 1 to 3 inches in diameter. Place on tray; cover with waxed paper. Melt chocolate as directed on package; cool 5 min. Spoon into small resealable plastic bag; cut small corner off bottom of bag. Trace over snowflake patterns with chocolate, rearranging patterns as needed to make a total of 35 chocolate snowflakes. Freeze 10 min. or until chocolate is firm. Carefully transfer snowflakes to plate; refrigerate until ready to use.

BEAT remaining dry pudding mix, sugar and milk in large bowl with whisk 2 min. Stir in COOL WHIP. Place 1 cake layer on plate; spread with jam, then ⅓ of the pudding mixture. Cover with remaining cake layer. Frost top and side of cake with remaining pudding mixture. Decorate with chocolate snowflakes. Keep refrigerated.

HIDDEN-CHOCOLATE SNOWFLAKE CAKE
Prepare using a chocolate cake mix and substituting 1 pkg. (3.9 oz.) JELL-O Chocolate Flavor Instant Pudding for the dry vanilla pudding mix added to the cake batter.

Sweets can be part of a balanced diet but remember to keep tabs on portions.

JELL-O Cookie Gems

Prep: 20 min. | Total: 1 hr 1 min. (incl. refrigerating) | Makes: 30 servings, 2 cookies each.

What you need

- 1 pkg. (8 oz.) **PHILADELPHIA** Cream Cheese, softened
- ¾ cup butter, softened
- 1 cup granulated sugar
- 2 tsp. vanilla
- 2¼ cups flour
- 1 pkg. (3 oz.) **JELL-O** Raspberry Flavor Gelatin
- ½ tsp. baking soda
- 2 Tbsp. powdered sugar

Make It

BEAT first 4 ingredients in large bowl with mixer until blended. Mix flour, dry gelatin mix and baking soda; gradually add to cream cheese mixture, mixing well after each addition. Refrigerate 30 min.

HEAT oven to 375°F. Roll dough into 60 (1-inch) balls. Place, 2 inches apart, on baking sheets sprayed with cooking spray.

BAKE 9 to 11 min. or until edges are lightly browned. Cool on baking sheets 2 min. Remove to wire racks; cool completely.

SPRINKLE with powdered sugar just before serving.

VARIATION
Prepare using JELL-O Lime Flavor Gelatin.

Snow-Covered Almond Crescents

Prep: 20 min. | Total: 1 hr 12 min. (incl. refrigerating) | Makes: 5 doz. or 30 servings, 2 cookies each.

What you need

- 1 pkg. (8 oz.) **PHILADELPHIA** Cream Cheese, softened
- ¾ cup butter, softened
- 1 cup granulated sugar
- 2 tsp. vanilla
- ½ tsp. almond extract
- 2¼ cups flour
- ½ tsp. baking soda
- 1 cup finely chopped **PLANTERS** Slivered Almonds
- ¾ cup powdered sugar

Make It

BEAT first 5 ingredients in large bowl with mixer until well blended. Add flour and baking soda; mix well. Stir in nuts. Refrigerate 30 min.

HEAT oven to 350°F. Roll dough into 60 (1-inch) balls; shape each into crescent shape. Place, 2 inches apart, on baking sheets. Flatten slightly.

BAKE 10 to 12 min. or until lightly browned. Cool 3 min. on baking sheets; transfer to wire racks. Cool completely. Sprinkle with powdered sugar.

Substitute
finely chopped
PLANTERS
Pecans for
the almonds.

Stunning Peanut Butter-Chocolate Layer Cake

Prep: 20 min. | Total: 1 hr 15 min. (incl. cooling) | Makes: 16 servings.

What you need

- 1 pkg. (2-layer size) yellow cake mix
- 2 pkg. (3.4 oz. each) **JELL-O** Vanilla Flavor Instant Pudding, divided
- 1 cup cold milk
- ½ cup **PLANTERS** Creamy Peanut Butter
- 6 oz. **BAKER'S** Semi-Sweet Chocolate, divided
- 1 pkg. (8 oz.) **PHILADELPHIA** Cream Cheese, cubed, softened
- ¼ cup butter, cut up, softened
- 3 cups powdered sugar
- ½ cup **PLANTERS** Lightly Salted Dry Roasted Peanuts, chopped

Make It

HEAT oven to 350°F.

LINE 13×9-inch pan with foil, with ends of foil extending over sides; spray with cooking spray. Prepare cake batter as directed on package, adding 1 pkg. dry pudding mix; beat 2 min. Pour into prepared pan. Bake 25 min. or until toothpick inserted in center comes out clean. Cool completely.

MEANWHILE, prepare filling and frosting. For filling, beat remaining dry pudding mix and milk in medium bowl with whisk 2 min. Stir in peanut butter until blended. For frosting, microwave 3 oz. chocolate in large microwaveable bowl on HIGH 1 min. or until melted, stirring after 30 sec. Add cream cheese and butter; beat with mixer until blended. Gradually beat in sugar. Use remaining chocolate to make chocolate curls as directed in How-To tip on page 18.

USE foil handles to lift cake from pan; cut crosswise in half. Place 1 cake half, top-side down, on plate; spread with peanut butter filling. Cover with remaining cake half, top-side up. Spread top and sides with chocolate frosting. Press nuts halfway up sides of cake; top with chocolate curls.

Starlight Mint Cake

Prep: 30 min. | Total: 4 hr 10 min. (incl. refrigerating) | Makes: 16 servings.

What you need

- 1 pkg. (2-layer size) white cake mix
- 1 cup boiling water
- 1 pkg. (3 oz.) **JELL-O** Cherry Flavor Gelatin
- 28 starlight mints, divided
- 3 oz. **BAKER'S** White Chocolate, melted
- 2 Tbsp. **BREAKSTONE'S** or **KNUDSEN** Sour Cream
- 2 drops red food coloring
- 2 cups thawed **COOL WHIP** Whipped Topping

Make It

PREPARE cake batter and bake as directed on package for 2 (9-inch) round cake layers. Cool cakes in pans 15 min. Pierce cakes with large fork at ½-inch intervals. Add boiling water to dry gelatin mix; stir 2 min. until completely dissolved. Pour over cakes. Refrigerate 3 hours.

HEAT oven to 350°F. Reserve 5 mints for later use. Place 12 of the remaining mints, about 4 inches apart, on parchment paper-covered baking sheet. Bake 5 min. or until mints are melted and each spreads out to 1½- to 2-inch circle. Remove from oven; cool completely before removing from parchment paper. Meanwhile, repeat with remaining 11 mints.

BLEND 5 reserved mints in blender until finely crushed; place in small bowl. Stir in melted chocolate, sour cream and food coloring.

DIP bottom of 1 cake pan in warm water 10 sec.; unmold onto serving plate. Spread cake with chocolate mixture. Unmold second cake layer; place on first layer. Frost with COOL WHIP. Decorate with melted mints. Keep refrigerated.

HOW TO BEND CANDY
To create a curvy effect on each melted candy, use a metal spatula to carefully remove melted candy from parchment while still warm and pliable. Slide candy onto the handle of a wooden spoon or any other object that will bend the candy. Cool completely before using to decorate cake.

Chocolate Plunge

Prep: 5 min. | Total: 5 min. | Makes: 1½ cups or 12 servings, 2 Tbsp. each.

What you need

- ⅔ cup light corn syrup
- ½ cup whipping cream
- 8 oz. **BAKER'S** Semi-Sweet Chocolate

Make It

MICROWAVE corn syrup and whipping cream in large microwavable bowl on HIGH 1½ min. or until mixture comes to boil. Add chocolate; stir until completely melted.

SERVE warm with cut-up fresh fruit, assorted cookies, pretzels and/or pound cake cubes.

CHOCOLATE-PEANUT BUTTER PLUNGE
Stir in ½ cup PLANTERS Peanut Butter along with chocolate.

CHOCOLATE-RASPBERRY PLUNGE
Stir in ¼ cup seedless raspberry jam along with chocolate.

MOCHA PLUNGE
Stir in 1 Tbsp. MAXWELL HOUSE Instant Coffee granules along with chocolate.

Tuxedo Cake

Prep: 30 min. | Total: 1 hr 40 min. (incl. cooling) | Makes: 16 servings.

What you need

- 1 pkg. (2-layer size) devil's food cake mix
- 1 pkg. (3.9 oz.) **JELL-O** Chocolate Instant Pudding
- 1½ pkg. (8 oz. each) **PHILADELPHIA** Cream Cheese, softened
- ½ cup butter, softened
- 1½ tsp. vanilla
- 6 cups powdered sugar
- ½ of 8-oz. tub **COOL WHIP** Whipped Topping (Do not thaw.)
- 2 oz. **BAKER'S** Semi-Sweet Chocolate Chocolate Curls (see How-To tip below)

Make It

HEAT oven to 350°F.

PREPARE cake batter and bake as directed on package for 2 (9-inch) round cake layers, blending dry pudding mix into batter before pouring into prepared pans. Cool 10 min. Loosen cakes from sides of pans with knife. Invert onto wire racks; gently remove pans. Cool cakes completely.

MEANWHILE, beat cream cheese, butter and vanilla in large bowl with mixer until blended. Gradually beat in sugar.

CUT each cake layer horizontally in half. Stack on plate, spreading ¾ cup cream cheese frosting between each layer. Spread remaining frosting onto top and sides of cake.

MICROWAVE COOL WHIP and chocolate in microwaveable bowl on HIGH 1½ min., stirring after 1 min.; stir until chocolate is completely melted and mixture is well blended. Cool 5 min. Pour over cake, letting excess drip down sides. Store cake in refrigerator. Garnish with Chocolate Curls before serving.

HOW TO MAKE CHOCOLATE CURLS

Microwave 3 oz. BAKER'S Semi-Sweet or White Chocolate and ½ tsp. shortening in microwaveable bowl on HIGH 30 sec.; stir. Microwave 30 to 40 sec. or until chocolate is almost melted; stir until completely melted. Spread into thin layer on baking sheet. Refrigerate 10 min. or until firm, but still pliable. Push metal spatula firmly across baking sheet, under chocolate, to make curls. (If chocolate is too firm, let stand a few minutes at room temperature; refrigerate if it becomes too soft.)

Chocolate Tres Leches Cake

Prep: 25 min. | Total: 2 hr (incl. refrigerating) | Makes: 16 servings.

What you need

- 1 pkg. (2-layer size) white cake mix
- 4 oz. **BAKER'S** Semi-Sweet Chocolate, divided
- 1 can (14 oz.) sweetened condensed milk
- 1 can (12 oz.) evaporated milk
- ½ cup **BREAKSTONE'S** or **KNUDSEN** Sour Cream
- 1 cup thawed **COOL WHIP** Whipped Topping

Make It

PREPARE cake batter and bake in 13×9-inch pan as directed on package. Cool cake in pan 10 min. Pierce cake with large fork at ½-inch intervals.

MELT 3 oz. chocolate as directed on package; set aside. Blend milks and sour cream in blender until smooth. Add melted chocolate; blend well. Pour over cake, re-piercing cake if necessary until milk mixture is absorbed. Refrigerate 1 hour. Meanwhile, make shavings from remaining chocolate.

FROST cake with COOL WHIP; top with chocolate shavings. Keep refrigerated.

Pass a vegetable peeler over the surface of the room-temperature chocolate to make shavings.

Chocolate-Candy Cane Cupcakes

Prep: 20 min. | Total: 1 hr 23 min. (incl. cooling) | Makes: 30 servings.

What you need

5 oz. **BAKER'S** Semi-Sweet Chocolate, divided

1 pkg. (2-layer size) chocolate cake mix

1 pkg. (3.9 oz.) **JELL-O** Chocolate Instant Pudding

1 cup **BREAKSTONE'S** or **KNUDSEN** Sour Cream

½ cup oil

½ cup water

4 eggs

6 small candy canes, crushed, divided

1 tub (8 oz.) **COOL WHIP** Whipped Topping, thawed

Make It

HEAT oven to 350°F.

CHOP 4 oz. chocolate; set aside. Beat next 6 ingredients with mixer until well blended. Stir in chopped chocolate and 2 Tbsp. candy. Spoon into 30 paper-lined muffin cups.

BAKE 20 to 23 min. or until toothpick inserted into centers comes out clean. Cool in pans 10 min.; remove to wire racks. Cool completely.

MELT remaining 1 oz. chocolate; cool slightly. Frost cupcakes with COOL WHIP; drizzle with chocolate. Sprinkle with remaining candy.

NOTE
Store frosted cupcakes in refrigerator.

You want to crush the candy to about a medium size. The candy inside the cake melts to give a peppermint flavor, and the candy on top provides a nice crunch.

Italian-Style Crème Brûlée

Prep: 15 min. | Total: 30 min. (incl. refrigerating) | Makes: 8 servings, ½ cup each.

What you need

- 2 pkg. (3.4 oz. each) **JELL-O** Vanilla Flavor Instant Pudding
- 1½ cups cold milk
- 1 cup cold half-and-half
- ½ cup Marsala wine
- ¼ cup packed brown sugar
- 1 Tbsp. powdered sugar
- 1 cup mixed fresh berries (blueberries, raspberries, blackberries)

Make It

BEAT dry pudding mixes, milk, half-and-half and wine with whisk 2 min.

POUR into shallow 1-qt. baking dish. Refrigerate 15 min.

HEAT broiler. Mix sugars; sprinkle over pudding. Broil, 6 inches from heat, 3 to 5 min. or until sugars are melted and caramelized. Let stand 5 min. Top with fruit. Serve immediately.

SUBSTITUTE
Substitute Madeira wine or additional milk for the Marsala wine.

Marty the "Mousse"

Prep: 20 min. | Total: 1 hr 20 min. (incl. refrigerating) | Makes: 18 servings.

What you need

- 16 oz. **BAKER'S** Semi-Sweet Chocolate, divided
- 1 pkg. (8 oz.) **PHILADELPHIA** Cream Cheese, softened
- ½ cup **PLANTERS** Walnut Halves

  Decorations: red candy-coated chocolate pieces, small candies

Make It

MELT 8 oz. chocolate. Beat cream cheese with mixer until creamy. Blend in melted chocolate. Refrigerate 1 hour or until firm.

SHAPE into 18 balls, using 4 tsp. chocolate mixture for each; place in single layer on waxed paper-covered baking sheet.

MELT remaining 8 oz. chocolate. Dip balls in chocolate, 1 at a time, turning to evenly coat each ball. Return to baking sheet. Press 2 nuts into top of each for the moose's antlers. Add decorations for the nose and eyes. Refrigerate until chocolate is firm.

SPECIAL EXTRA
Add 1 to 2 tsp. of your favorite extract, such as peppermint, rum or almond, to chocolate mixture before shaping into balls.

No-Bake Chocolate Cream Cupcakes

Prep: 10 min. | Total: 1 hr 10 min. (incl. refrigerating) | Makes: 2 servings, 1 cupcake each.

What you need

- ½ cup thawed **COOL WHIP** Whipped Topping, divided
- 2 oz. (¼ of 8-oz. pkg.) **PHILADELPHIA** Cream Cheese, softened
- 1 oz. **BAKER'S** Semi-Sweet Chocolate, melted, cooled
- 1 Tbsp. powdered sugar
- 8 vanilla wafers

Make It

MIX ¼ cup COOL WHIP, cream cheese, melted chocolate and sugar until well blended.

PLACE 2 of the wafers on bottom of each of 2 paper-lined medium muffin cups. Cover with 1 Tbsp. COOL WHIP mixture. Repeat layers. Top evenly with remaining COOL WHIP. Cover.

REFRIGERATE at least 1 hour.

Garnish with a sprinkling of unsweetened cocoa just before serving.

Prepare using reduced-fat vanilla wafers and PHILADELPHIA Neufchâtel Cheese.

Raspberry Kisses

Prep: 10 min. | Total: 10 min. | Makes: 2 doz. or 12 servings, 2 cookie sandwiches each.

What you need

48 vanilla wafers

½ cup (½ of 8-oz. tub) **PHILADELPHIA** Cream Cheese Spread

¼ cup seedless raspberry jam or preserves

1 Tbsp. powdered sugar

Make It

SPREAD each of 24 wafers with 1 tsp. cream cheese spread; top with ½ tsp. jam.

COVER with remaining wafers to make sandwiches.

SPRINKLE with sugar.

NOTE
For crisper texture, serve immediately. Or for a cake-like texture, place in airtight container and store in refrigerator overnight before serving.

HOW TO STORE
Store leftovers in airtight container in refrigerator.